Rosepetals
towards memory...

by Nina Freedlander Gibans

Rosepetals
towards memory...

by Nina Freedlander Gibans

Copyright © 2018

Cover Design by Jared Bendis

ISBN — 9781626130968

Published by ATBOSH Media ltd.
Cleveland, Ohio, USA

http://www.atbosh.com

Some context...

On May 10th 2018, Jim Gibans died.

In April of 2018, when Jim's health started to decline, Nina wrote to him, she wrote him poetry. She wrote him a poem almost every day.

And she read them to him.

Nina is no stranger to poetry, she has been writing all her life.

Jim had written to her as well. For the over 60 years Jim and Nina were together, they spent very little time apart. But when they were apart, Jim wrote to her. At their bedside Nina keeps a box of over 100 letters that Jim wrote to her when he was studying in England in 1954/1955.

She even has the letter that Jim wrote to her father asking for her hand in marriage.

It's a lovely letter. You have to read it for yourself.

When Jim passed away, we were just finishing work on *Celebrating The Soul of Cleveland*, Nina's love letter to her city. And Nina decided to put together this book of poetry in time for Jim's Celebration of Life.

And that is the context.

But wait there's more.

The images of Jim and Nina on the cover are from a work commissioned from Chris Pekoc for their 50th anniversary.

The red sculpture on the front was commissioned from Fred Schmidt in honor of their 45th anniversary and Jim's 70th birthday.

It was Jim's favorite piece.

Every year Jim and Nina would design a holiday card. Jim would draw a picture and Nina would write a poem.

This is their card from 1999:

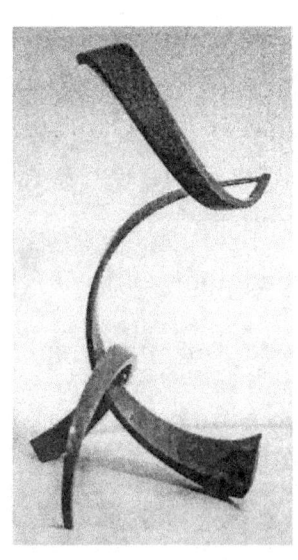

"Sometimes we do not share dried petals in our scrapbooks; we dig deeper for times forgotten. Until we smell gardenias."

From "Stories from the Gardeners"
"18 Gardens and Their Gardeners"
Nina Gibans, 1999

Greetings for a special season
Nina and Jim Gibans
December, 1999

"Dancing to 45/70"
Commissioned for celebrations
Fred Schmidt, 1999

There is so much joy in their cards and letters.
So many stories, so many memories.

> We crossed America's element,
> impressionistically.
> Changes in a settled place
> seen through twelve blue eyes;
> the second act of a play—
> people in a slightly different setting
> of greater complication.
> We are pioneers in our own way—
> in from the West
> and six years in our own green valley.
> Settled and always moving,
> our friends are with us.
> Hello, 1965
>
> Nina and Jim Gibans
> David, Jonathan, Amy, Elisabeth

Jared Bendis
Publisher & Friend
July 2018

james d. gibans

Derby Hall
North Mossley Hill Road
Liverpool 18, England
Tuesday, November 9th, 1954

Dear Dr. Freedlander,

    This letter is a most difficult one to write, the more so because you already know what reason lies behind it. But on the other hand, it makes me very happy to be writing this to you. And, I must admit, I find it a bit amusing putting you through the same most unusual situation twice!

    You know that Nina and I are very much in love, and wish to become man and wife. Before I left for England, Nina and I had talked over the matter carefully, and had decided to hold off any decision until we had seen each other again after this long period of being apart. But my absence from her has all the more convinced me of my love for her, and she admits of the same feelings. Moreover, external circumstances, as I believe she has explained to you, have entered the scene and have acted as a catalyst to our desire to be married. And I know that even if we had hesitated until July, our feelings would not have changed, and, indeed, shall not change.

    To extoll the virtues of your daughter to you would be most superfluous, for you yourself know them as well as,- indeed, better than, I. Let it just be said that in Nina is everything and more that I have ever hoped to have in a wife, that we seem to have so very much in common, and that I love her.

    I cannot promise her happiness, but shall do everything in my power to make her happy. I cannot promise her security, but shall do as much as I can to give us a comfortable home, though it may be a number of years before I can begin to acheive that end. There is yet a long ways for me to go before I can feel competent enough, and in fact, be recognized, as any sort of architect, and where this search will lead us I cannot truthfully say. But I think I can promise an interesting search. I cannot promise her a perfect husband, and I know she realizes that already (indeed, she is probably cooking up schemes right now to reform me!), but I shall do all I can to be a good partner. With Army service still ahead of me, we shall have far from an ideal first few years together, but I know that we would rather be together during that time than apart. I fully realize that I can't even say what is to happen to Nina and myself after a honeymoon, which is a very poor way to begin a marriage, but I think we would rather start out that way now than not start out at all.

With all this in mind, I humbly ask for your permission to marry your daughter. Please give us your blessing; have patience with us; and have faith in us. We shall not disappoint you.

Yours most sincerely,

james d. gibans
Derby Hall
North Mossley Hill Road
Liverpool 18, England

Dr. S. O. Freedlander
19201 Van Aken Blvd.
Shaker Heights 22,
Ohio,
U. S. A.

BY AIR MAIL
PAR AVION

April 2, 2018

For friend Richard
Cranial creases
Beautiful lines

Creative thinking
In oranges, yellows, reds
A little purple.
New forms like old friends
we see and we remember.
grey stone
softened
by years of kindness.

April 4, 2018

If I were not here
I would be there
Where?
Looking at the still frozen lake and wondering
      about winter/spring
I do that every year
Laughing at myself still warming by the fire
      before the sun shows its summer face
But it's April.
Which makes it easy to slide back and forth
with procrastination, indecision, and the lazier
      moods
Like a trombone badly played facing the wind.
I am looking forward—only forward
To twist in the sunlight of better ideas
Because I am not where I want to be.

April 5, 2018

Telling friends of a death
Finishing touches on the portrait
In greys and bursts of color
Likenesses curiously debated as observers,
Confidantes, story-tellers come from the
        crevices
Each with a piece of the fabric sewing a blanket
        of truths
corals changing color; crustaceans peeling
        skins;
fall leaves in VT; quartets of violins, trios
of cellos and pianos; rooms filled with quotes.
we read our friends through the chapters of
        days
bandage our common disgust with obscenities
by skimming the worst words, not readable for
        our souls.

April 6, 2018

Rogue life
led by the therapy dog
Wandering the streets and then into our lives.
Licking his wounds and ours
His treats our treat
Patience and a brush of his approval
His tail.

April 7, 2018

Ever since Bachelard dug into my roots
Every room has staged some part of my life
Every day
With patterns for learning
And loving
And hovering and seeking
And believing.

April 8, 2018

Shades and shadows
wall paintings
On my room
My history
A hand, a head
Hieroglyphic.

April 9, 2018

I never wanted to go that way
I marked my life in space
Lined up questions with answers
Explored ideas reasonably
And steadily.
The roses were many reds —
Matching the dahlias, the lush pinks
Parading across the border cushioning
The rich perfumed soil
Until I brought them inside to garnish tables.
When I served chicken marsala with matching
       wine.
To hosts of friends for sixty years.

April 10, 2018

I never wanted to go that way
I marked my life with
Delicious days
Groceries a treasure hunt for inspiration
Red raspberries in white Arzberg saucers
Well-tested vinegar and olive oil for delicate
    greens
Chocolate soufflé light and feathery,
My mother's teaching
Turkey moist to perfection
My mother's teaching
Laughter and fun
My mother's teaching.

April 11, 2018

I never wanted to go that way
Even now I check the blueprints in my mind
Laden with red pen marks for improvement.
Sometimes when I put the pen in my pocket
I leave a stain of honor —don't all architects?
I am always making a list of final checkpoints
Edges of shelves, door jambs. Entryways,
Adjusting mirror, towel dispensers,
Are the lights bright enough?,
Do the shades allow enough sun?
I am no longer sure, but the answer is in the
       looking.
Just keep looking.

April 12, 2018

Recollections in jazz
My head bumps along with melody and
 syncopation.
Like the lives we lead—stirring hopes
And resolution.
The songs of living
Feet — loaded with life,
Sole to soul.

April 13, 2018

Sitting outside for the first time this Spring
Winter has not quite given in.
Is tepid, testing
validity?

April 14, 2018

I never wanted it to go this way
I believed In myself
And others
Now I am not sure of myself
And others are not sure of me.
The dog still licks my hand
Because he likes treats
Just like me.
Soft voices
Feather touches
Velvet massage
And us.

April 15, 2018

I never wanted to go this way
This is too menacing
for everyone. They knew me as a conqueror
sword in hand, brave and gentle all at once,
Robin Hood was ok, but Monty Python is more
      my style
I laughed a lot.

April 16, 2018

I never went without my Leica
European splendor
City glories
My children – being themselves
Raising puppies (5 kinds over 15 years),
    snakes, rabbits
Gerbils, turtles, and a cat.
Pied pipers to the animal world.
Details selected
others put the whole together.

April 17, 2018

Roses from my father
Herbs I can eat
Color for every room
Dig away worries
I cut flowers and share perennials
I take pride
Getting to know people
The sun is warm ideas grow
Tales are wrapped in the cutting shears
This moment belongs to us.

April 18, 2018

I never wanted to go this way
I travel with Handel operas, Dizzy jazz,
Subjecting myself to splendor
Filling my joy
On the way to work.

April 19, 2018

Matching socks set my day forward
On pace
Helps me think of color
Bromide for work
Patterns make sense
Albers every day
Color codes my life.

April 20, 2010

I never wanted to go like this
I was open to options
Reading without interruption
Tuners set for listening, not fixing
Simple food –colorful, well-chosen down the
 street
From my mushroom friends or Kate's Fish
Or new asparagus
Young corn
Raspberry bread from Michael
Bartering meat with Savory
Years of managing food relationships
My friends in food
But Henry's my flower friend. Shared dahlia
 bulbs.

April 21, 2018

I never wanted to go this way
never in Spring when the bulbs come up
and surprise me from last Fall
I check out the buds
And design my travel route for beauty
The neighborhood awakens to emergence
With the growers, and the gatherers
Stories.

April 22, 2018

I never wanted to go this way
My day comes in different colors
Yellow stuns my steps on the sidewalks of life
Dashes to lighten trees, separates the branches
With positive upward peaks
Bounces my energy
Through my body light.

April 23, 2018

I never wanted to go this way
Smile upon the famous trip to Shaw
Forgot my passport
A busload of friends vouching for my existence
The border guard threatening
In their "Oh Mr." gruff
Just enough to sound official.
Shaw was always worth it
Buried on the festive flowered street
Criss-crossroad to wineries,
Here's to Shaw, the brilliant troublemaker
Making my time worth the risk.

April 24, 2018

I didn't want to go this way
I always packed carefully,
Fitting not stuffing
Folding not throwing
Planning by the inch.
Ordaining the ins and outs of trip clothing
According to suitcase fit or color.

April 25, 2018

I didn't want to go this way
I'd write my way out if I could
Postmarked yesterday
No one sends mail anymore anyway
And I am not a Facebook guy
And I didn't want to go through another
        election
So I am leaving now.

April 26, 2018

I didn't want to go this way
I still laugh at architectural jokes
The spoofs on us —how we acted or dressed, or
      our daily habits;
the ink splotch in the pocket because I forgot
      the cap was off the pen;
the memory trip of me placed in montages —
      fantastic array of places that
all architects have memorized all over the
      world;
Laugh at our 60 year-old Paul McCobb
      furniture
our red Saarinen chair.
I lived with them happily.
They're me.

April 27, 2018

I never wanted to go this way
Drawing the lines of life
On a gurney
The handwriting was on the wall, on the rails,
    the ceiling
On the floor. When I fell, I stumbled into the
    end.
In my pocket is a little piece of paper left over
    from dinner
Got our names on it and my signature.

April 28, 2018

I never wanted to go this way
By choice we were of that mind;
sorry to disappoint everyone
just let me be myself to the end.
I tried. Did the punch list for our building
the building is very good.
I examined every crease of wood
Every rail, every shelf, doorknob.
I corrected mistakes (in my head of course)
Was going to tell you about them when we met.
Soon.

April 29, 2018

I always wanted to play trills on my piano
Perfectly just like the melodies I hear
Every day. Our being together was a melody
Deep harmonies of living
In the same world and particularly peacefully
While buffering challenges
We both had.
But going my way would have been different
And measured.

April 30, 2018

I never wanted to go that way
Or to climb Mt Everest
Or ski on slippery slopes
Or skim mountain tops in South America.
I just wanted to keep my promises to myself
To come home to love every day.

April 31, 2018

I never wanted to go that way
Music must pave my way
Leave love? Leave my soul in the gardens,
and the sunset tomorrow.

Wondering
Whispering
Withering

What Am I Doing Here?

I never wanted to go this way.
What am I doing lying around
Unsettled
Blind and deaf
On the floor-mattress?
I examined the building in my checklist of today
Looking for best practices as they say
I strode the halls and tested doors while visiting
      people
Tested door jambs, cupboard shelves, railings
For perfection.
60 years
Blind date pick bonanza
Weedless top soil pick
I was a perfectionist after all (just for myself);
Planting on time,
Roses right red,
Chicken marinade in proper wine
Cooking seriously
Proper knives and forks, dishes
From our honeymoon.

Jim in the garden. Photograph by Michael Loderstedt.

The Sunlight Tinkers with The Day

The sunlight tinkers with the day
Leaf tones , like teabags partially wet
Are neither today or tonight.
Building greys and brown city poles stand
      sentinel as the last sun glares
into the glass windows that soon will be night
      black
with time rolling in.
You are not here to agree
I will speak for both of us
Because I have known you so many moments of
      time like this.
They are gentle and loving, smiling with the
      sunlit leaf.

About the Author

Some more context...
   Poetry has been a life venture for Nina.

- At Laurel School. Her translations from Latin and in English class went mostly unappreciated.
- In the presence of poets her entire life. Including studies with Horace Gregory (Sarah Lawrence College), Louis Zukofsky (San Francisco Poetry Center), Vincent McHugh (San Francisco — Retired chair of Federal Writing Project, NYC), a workshop with Alicia Ostriker, and communication with Naomi Shihab Nye, Robert Pinsky, Alberta Turner. Friend of Richard Howard, Cleveland native Pulitzer Prize MacArthur Award winner.— encouraging encounters.
- Read in San Francisco as part of the group working with Vincent McHugh in bars and on the stage as a fore-act to Allen Ginsberg's performance.
- Active with Poet's League of Cleveland.
- Publications: *And So I Must Imagine* (XLibris 2009). Co-editor with Mary Weems and Larry Smith of Cleveland Poetry Scenes: *A Panorama and Anthology* (Bottom Dog Press 2008) Piloted at John Hay High School and Shaker Heights Middle School and Cleveland Public Libraries. *18 Gardens and their Gardeners* with Michael Loderstedt, photographer, 1999 an Ohio Arts Council Art Project Grant.
- Taught creative writing at The Cleveland Museum of Art in East Cleveland arts project.
- Co-Director, *Silver Apples of the Moon* project asking for community response to poetry and art — with Shaker Heights Public Library, Cleveland Public Library, & The Cleveland Museum of Art, & the. Book edited by Neal Chandler, Cleveland State University.
- Read in museums, bookstores, and libraries in Cleveland.

"we are connected underneath the seafloor of our psyches" from *Poetry and Healing: Some Moments of Wholeness* by Alicia Ostriker in the *American Poetry Review*, March/April 2018.

www.ingramcontent.com/pod-product-compliance
Lightning Source LLC
Chambersburg PA
CBHW050047080526
44586CB00014B/1500